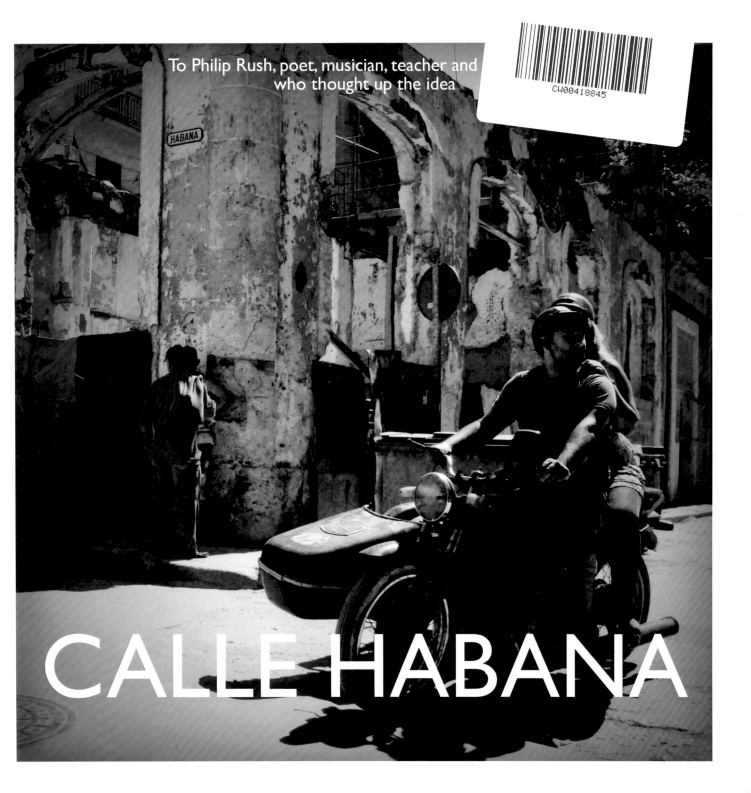

To Philip Rush, poet, musician, teacher and
who thought up the idea

HABANA

CW00418845

CALLE HABANA

THE FLOATING ISLAND

Brillando contra el sol y contra los poetas Heberto Padilla

There it is, the long prow
of the Caribbean, charging to break
the map's complexion.
It is a key, a crocodile, a hook,
an uncoiling question,
a stretch of sinews catching
dribbles from the continent
under which it will, forever, float.

The island mouth is smiling
or frowning, who can tell,
stuffed with waning intentions,
sugarcane and sand.

Such a little place, such
an island listing against sorrow
in the middle of the ocean's gut,
playing make believe
queen of brine, dressing up in green
and calling forth its poets for praise,
its leaders for chesty boasts,
inventing for itself a pantheon
of tropical saints, a vast
and profound literature,
an epic history to rival Rome's.

There it is, pretending it shimmers
over the heads of its people,
denying the terror it feels
when no one listens, denying
that it is always almost drowning,
that it cannot help anyone, least
of all itself, that it is only
a strip of dirt between morning and night,
between what will be and what was,
between the birth of hope
and the death of desire.

THE LOVE OF BLONDES

I don't know what I would be
if there were no Cuba,
if there were no childhood,
no malecón or José Martí,
no sharks in the water, no hot car
seat sticking to the underthighs
midafternoon, no Jaimanitas where we fished,
la Playa where we swam,
no Constellation gunning its engines
over the Tropic of Cancer,
if we hadn't left behind a frown,
a sweet and sour pill,
the arroz con frijoles of politics and laughter.

What if I woke one morning
and I was Serbian or Senegalese
or star-spangled American?
When I think everything is in control
I remember the day my father
took me to a ball game in el Cerro
- Habana against Almendares -
and he put five on the home team
and bought me a peanut cone
and I saw the Cuban flag waving
in front of all that blue sky.
I was the happiest boy on earth,
I thought I had entered eternity,
I thought el Cerro was Paradise
and the ball players were angels
and God was Bicicleta, the obese
ball retriever, JJ the bet taker,
a manic John the Baptist.

And then, I remember, as JJ ran
to the numbers man waving money
and stumbling, the blonde appeared,
sliding down the steps to the box seats,
tall and tanned and movie-liquid,
making the vendors stop their hawking
and the men in the stands
hold their arguments and fat Bicicleta
turn away from foul balls.
Over the stadium came a silence
it had never known, every man there joined
in admiration, adulation
and longing for the blonde in blue
just then sitting down, letting the sun
illuminate the freckles on her shoulder.
And I, we, became blasphemers, idolaters,
Bicicleta paling beside this sun-goddess,
this saint of salivation, this Helen of elation.
From that point on Paradise
was no longer el Cerro but the steps
she trod, the dress she wore,
the chair she sat on, the country
of her birth, the polis of her pubis.

I ate of the fruit of baseball and beauty.
The land faded, happiness disappeared
and I realized my loss –
el Cerro forgotten, JJ in a wheelchair,
Bicicleta dead and I don't know
what would happen if there was no Cuba
and I were someone else,
living in Dakar or Indianapolis
next door to the blonde,
she always calling me over for coffee
and I obliging.

CALLE DE LA AMARGURA

In Havana there is a street called Calle de la Amargura or Street of Bitterness

On the Street of Bitterness
a man runs from the rain
arms raised into the next imagination.

A woman sits head down
on the stoop of a house
where her indiscretions
fly about like butterflies.

All songs end,
memories soar over rooftops,
an eyelid swells with desire.

On the Street of Bitterness,
Calle de la Amargura, there are boys
scratching their tongues,
they dare not speak, they await
their turn in the line of understanding.

On that street
a daughter is dying.
Her father searches for a cure
and finds instead the pillar of his wife,
covered with lizard scales,
melting with the rain.

On the Street of Bitterness,
Calle de la Amargura, no one is surprised
at the awful taste of Paradise.

EX LIBRIS

Childhood was Cervantes,
adulthood flared with Hemingway.

I look for death in every book,
intertextual, salivary:

what the ocean says
and says again and then forgets.

ARS POETICA

What do you know
about poetry?

What do you know
about the last grain

of the last meal of rice
on the universe of your plate?

HAVANA DREAM

The red eye blinks and it is you
(in between the rain)

out of the crumbling rooms,
a note played on the piano,

a salt wind off the ocean,
lonely, refracted (you).

NEW TANGO

Not those old places
(not the strain of abandon).

You want to rob the present
for childhood, the streets

for the crust of a dream
where your voice comes back in a bell.

SMOKE AND MIRRORS IN HAVANA

The sea in its immensity
is telling a story.

Here is darkness (long,
long train through the night).

There under the carpet, grandmother
dust, grandfather consequence.

END OF THE AFFAIR

Funny how the fun collapses,
archaic, blended into threnody.

Funny how we dream of hoping
and go back to the books,

the dusty shelves. (Funny how)
our patience lapses.

AT THE BLUE NOTE

Sometimes in the heat of the snow
you want to cry out

for pleasure or pain like a bell.
And you wind up holding each other,

listening to the in-between
despite the abyss at the edge of the table.

Hell. Mulgrew Miller plays like a big
bad spider, hands on fire, the piano

trembling like crystal,
the taste and smell of a forest under water.

The bartender made us a drink
with butterfly wings and electric wire.

Bitter cold outside, big silence,
a whale growing inside us.

OUT OF THE GAME

after Herberto Padilla

Say goodbye to the poet!
He's got nothing to do here.
He doesn't play the game.
He's not enthusiastic.
His message lacks clarity.
He's not impressed by miracles even.
All he does is complain.
He always finds something to object to.

Say goodbye to this character!
Move this grump to a corner.
He wears dark glasses under the early sun,
his ill humor spills into summer.

Wandering has always seduced him
as well as the beautiful catastrophes
of time without History.
Besides, he is old fashioned.
He likes that old man Armstrong.
If he has to, he'll hum a Pete Seeger tune
and even sing the Guantanamera.

But no one can make him
open his mouth.
No one can make him smile
when the spectacle begins
and the clowns jump into the act.

When the cockatoos confuse love with terror
and the stage groans
and the horns blow and the drum beats
everyone else jumps,
leans to one side,
shuffles back, smiles,
speaks

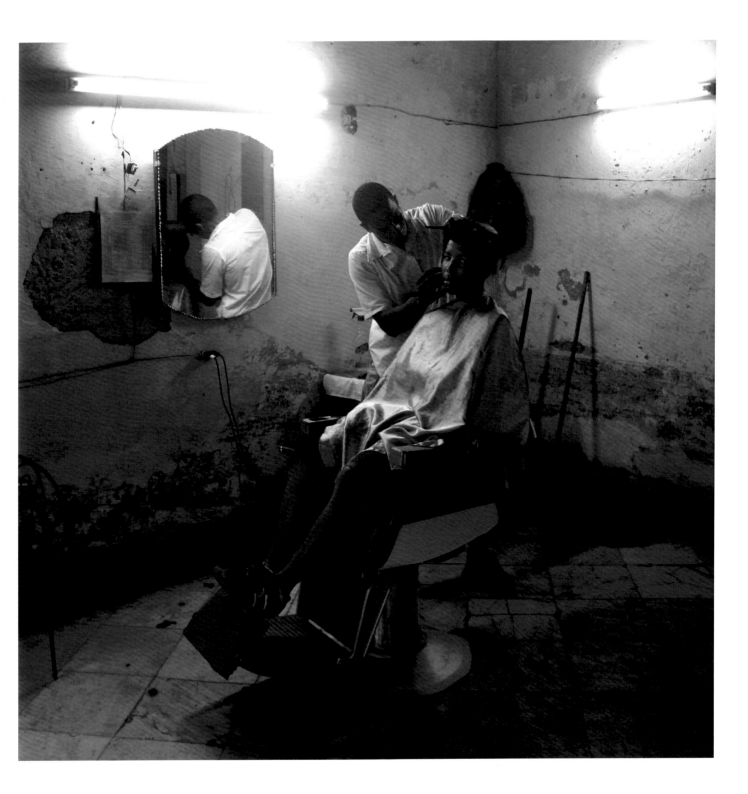

well, yes,
of course, yes
definitely yes…

Everyone else dances well,
dances smartly,
the way they are told to dance.
Say goodbye to this creature!
He's got nothing to do here.

SAINT OF THE FOREST

Homage to Lydia Cabrera

You want to kiss the moon? You want to write the truth?
It is no washing of deception in the ocean of this world.
The saints remake this so. The sand sucks up the water,
lets it go. And the coconut bares its shape, no matter
the answers of the night, the milk dripping from the stars.
The river is dark water, everyone knows that, it doesn't
reveal itself like a lagoon or that big tree you tried
to hide behind, that lie. The moon is not a girl, the river's
not a man. The fish wait for your lips when you're
in muck. They taste first, then they bite.
The saints open the road to great sinning, sixteen hard
boiled eggs in a cross. You have to be cared for
when stepping on the shadow bigger than the tree.
There are horses here and there's a field you never go in
where they grow pieces of you, shards and slivers
of what you're born to. The temper suits you.
All the time you remember the slow insect climbing
up the wall to the sun, spiky legs, long
feelers clicking, saying something to you,
going back to the day your aunt cut the water
snake in half with her machete,
back to the mosquito that sucked your blood,
back to your mama's big wet breasts. Is that it?
Your mind's a mess, can't tell the difference between
lie and truth, between what you want and what you won't,
tenderly or with a rock falling on your head.
You've got to learn the biscuit and the cream of it, choke
juice coming out your mouth. And when you come to dream
you know the difference between mystery and sin.
All you think about is in your suitcase, bunch of smoke.

Row out to the middle of the ocean and talk to the waves,
the foamy part. When you speak their language you learn
lie doesn't matter, truth doesn't matter. Singing.
Rocking. Watching the moon go to her place,
way up behind the sun, behind the milk your mama gave.
You solitude, you company, you all that stays.

SAINT OF THE ROYAL PALM

The sacred tree belongs to the Lord Changó.
It is the straightest and the tallest
given to inklings of grandeur,
draws the lightening from the sky.
In the savanna there are many
places to lie down and die,
places to watch the saints
frolic, laugh at humans,
have sex and sleep. I was a child
down there. I saw what goes on –
the boys mounting the girls,
the girls splashing water on themselves.
Big and open, red and hot
midday. I learned the toad song
and the beetle song and the bull song
and the song of rain and puddles.
I learned there is no man to stand up
to Changó. He is the chief of heaven
but he lives on earth. You don't want
him angry. That's why you offer him
everything – the goat,
the rooster, your fattest child. Not
that he's asked. His message
is lightning and thunder. You want
to kiss his feet? He's got no feet.
You want to hold his hand?
He's got no hand. He's all trunk
and hair – those big green fronds.
He's all eye, watching you awake
and asleep. In the savanna,
in the hills, in the city where it's
hard and dry. The royal palm
standing over the cane fields,
his voice in thunder, his face on fire.

AZUL

Color that spills into twilight like honey,
the moonlight gold on the bed,
old glint of the goddess torn loose,
a cry polished by distance, ship
we sail on through the dark passes.

Color that joins the days
(two lovers twining
like trees by our window)
color the wine of the sea,
silence under our breathing (color the heart)
clean as the sheets of our loving,
certain as stone, deep
as the well of our grace.

TO THE LOVER

after Carmen Matute

Feeling my way
through your skin
I forgot the parched skin
of my country,
I stopped wandering the roads,
never reached the towns,
ignored the hunger and violence.
Instead I drowned in a bottomless orgasm,
I turned into a seashell,
a turtle
hiding in the depths of the house.
I lived without purpose,
chirping away like the cricket of the fable.
My house without doors and windows.
My monumental selfishness
on me like a chrysalis.
But our loving grew –
our loving, a dialogue of years,
kisses, blows, and bites –
until it became a huge basket of bread,
enough for everyone.
You know it, love.
Today, under our sheets,
I find all the women and the men
and the children of our city.
We agree, then:
from now on,
let us make room for everyone!

POSTSCRIPT ONE

Some days ago, Carlos Ordoñez sent me a draft of *Calle Habana*, containing his images and my poetry. When I opened the file, memories rushed at me in a flood, memories of my childhood in Havana and of my return after a 38-year absence. I was so excited I immediately called a friend and told her about the treasure I'd received. Later that day, looking at the proofs with greater calm, I realized that the blend of my texts and Carlos' photos resulted in something fresh and original that had little to do with memory and instead arose out of the synesthetic relationship between people and place, place and image, image and word. I'd never seen the city of my birth in quite this way. Carlos, the English son of an exile from Franco's Spain, was showing me, an exile from Castro's Cuba, the way to join the countries of sorrow and distance, grief and joy, via the dance of poetry, photography, and compassion.

Carlos Ordoñez's photographs are stunning in the way that unalloyed images are stunning: the eye doesn't judge, nor does it claim the territory of the righteous, for whom the sanitized vision is the primary measure of the subject. Carlos's eye sees, in other words, not what it wants to see, but what the light presents—the interplay of form and shadow: a room of peeling walls and immaculate harlequin floor; the movement of a man (a ghost, a threat?) past the bare shoulders of a young woman; a barbershop in which a barber still cuts hair fifty years past elegance; a street in ruins, reminiscent of a war zone, except the only war here is the one that time always wins. The ultimate work of the artist is to let things and people speak for themselves, to leave his interpretive "I" behind and let the physical eye take over. To achieve this, both grace and decency are necessary, qualities that Carlos exhibits in abundance. It is my good fortune to have my poems accompany his images.

Pablo Medina, 14 February 2013

POSTSCRIPT TWO

I first met Pablo Medina in June, 2011. A convoluted road drew us together to celebrate the life and work of Federico Garcia Lorca, on the 75th anniversary of his murder during the Spanish Civil War. That encounter provided me with the opportunity to reflect – through Pablo's poetry – on my own efforts to construct a coherent 'sense of self', as the son of immigrant parents. Their displacement. like his, wasn't simply a question of distance, but of ideology, and loss of personal and collective identity - dimensions so thoughtfully addressed by Pablo's writings.

Reading them set me in a particular place: of isolation and 'polished distance', even from those circles I'd rather like to be a full part of. Conditions for any authentic belonging involve free play between 'ego' and 'social' – fluid like sea and Malecon, poetry and bodily secretions, 'son' and rum. A 'floating island', Pablo, nevertheless, yearns for more, much more, exemplified by his line of travel between curvaceous, loving exaltation and painful, bitter refrain – expressing the desire of the exile to 'make room for everyone'. It brought back the child sitting in meetings each Sunday, listening in on fiery debates on property relations and economic self-management, overlaid with a terrible sense of loss.

Pablo's experiences on his trip to Cuba in 1999 – with all the emotion and trauma involved in a search for affirmation of early memories – also put me in touch with the heavy sweat I lay in, as the midnight sleeper slipped across the border into Spain on the first visit in 1979. The 'ruins' of memories Pablo found then in Havana, are both outwardly real (as photographs attest) and really internalised (something it took a third visit to Cuba to begin to appreciate). His memories are grounded in concrete family ties, specific places and moments; mine, by contrast, in the 'idea' of living with inherent imperfection – unreliable as 'memory', but sufficiently absorbing in all its possibilities to last a lifetime walking, talking, dreaming down every Calle Habana in the company of Pablo's poetry.

Pablo's visual imagination, way with language (you should hear him read his poetry), and humanity have made this collaboration to put his words and my pictures together, a very special experience.

Carlos Ordoñez, 25 February 2013